WILLIAM ROWE

NEW ART DECO BORDERS AND MOTIFS

DOVER PUBLICATIONS, INC.
NEW YORK

Copyright © 1984 by Dover Publications, Inc.
All rights reserved under Pan American and International Copyright Conventions.

Published in Canada by General Publishing Company, Ltd., 30 Lesmill Road, Don Mills, Toronto, Ontario.
Published in the United Kingdom by Constable and Company, Ltd., 10 Orange Street, London WC2H 7EG.

New Art Deco Borders and Motifs is a new work, first published by Dover Publications, Inc., in 1984.

DOVER *Pictorial Archive* SERIES

New Art Deco Borders and Motifs belongs to the Dover Pictorial Archive Series. Up to ten illustrations may be used on any one project or in any single publication free and without special permission. Whenever possible, include a credit line indicating the title of this book, author and publisher. Please address the publisher for permission to make more extensive use of illustrations in this book than that authorized above.
The republication of this book in whole is prohibited.

Manufactured in the United States of America
Dover Publications, Inc., 31 East 2nd Street, Mineola, N.Y. 11501

Library of Congress Cataloging in Publication Data

Rowe, William, 1946–
New art deco borders and motifs.

(Dover pictorial archive series)
1. Art deco—Themes, motives. 2. Borders, Ornamental (Decorative arts) I. Title. II. Series.
NK1396.A76R68   1984   745.4'442   84-8015
ISBN 0-486-24709-0 (pbk.)

PUBLISHER'S NOTE

In this, William Rowe's ninth book for Dover, the artist continues to give fresh interpretations of the Art Deco style. His interest in the revival of the decorative idiom of the Twenties and Thirties dates back at least to his *Original Art Deco Designs* (22567-4) published by Dover in 1973. Rowe prefers to call the style Art Moderne, but has agreed to let us apply the more widely used term to the title of his book.

The present volume is comprised of 72 striking designs masterfully executed in pen and ink. The plates are primarily based on geometric patterns, in the manner of the Jazz Age, but Rowe varies the play of circles, squares and other abstract forms with floral motifs of the kind that have enchanted browsers in his *Flora and Fauna Fantasies* (1976, 23289-1).

The plates are presented in five suites, each beginning with a pair of designs (or in the case of the first suite, a single composition) centered on a numeral. These introductory plates state the visual premise of the suite, and those that follow give variations on the theme. The artist has taken evident pleasure in the progressive transformations of pattern and field, and his enjoyment will be shared by those who flip through these pages in search of a usable border or for the sheer delight of the designs themselves.

One of the basic motifs in this collection is the combination of the cross with a circle or square at the intersection of the axes, an arrangement reminiscent of the "God's eye" of Mexican folk art. This pattern undergoes many metamorphoses. Here the cross is doubled; there the superimposed figures are repeated or transmuted. By using stippling and reticulation for varied tonal effects, Rowe adds vitality to the fundamental monochrome geometry of the designs.

In the second suite, the artist introduces floral and foliate elements, choosing such irregularly shaped flowers as irises, orchids and honeysuckles, in charming contrast to the underlying symmetry of the geometric backgrounds. Some of the most vigorous effects are derived from the interplay of light and dark on variegated leaves.

Like his previous books in the Pictorial Archive Series, Rowe's *New Art Deco Borders and Motifs* offers designers, illustrators and craftspeople superb graphics that will find ready use in any number of applications and will inspire others to take part in the exciting current revival of the Art Deco style. The art will reproduce easily and cleanly, and it is copyright-free. Rowe's many admirers will revel in this addition to his oeuvre.

1

11

25

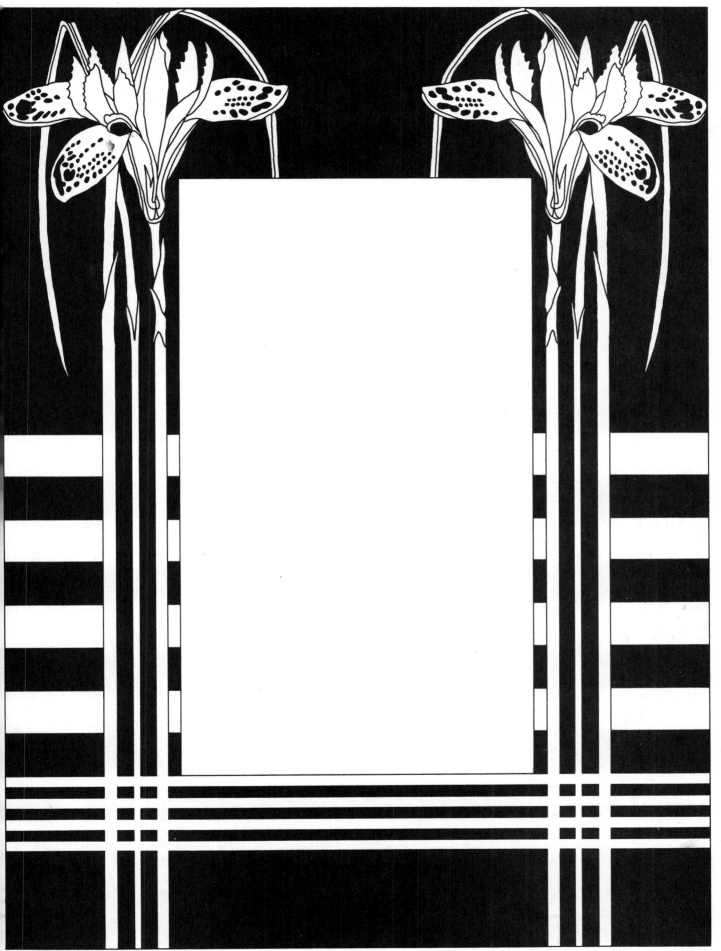

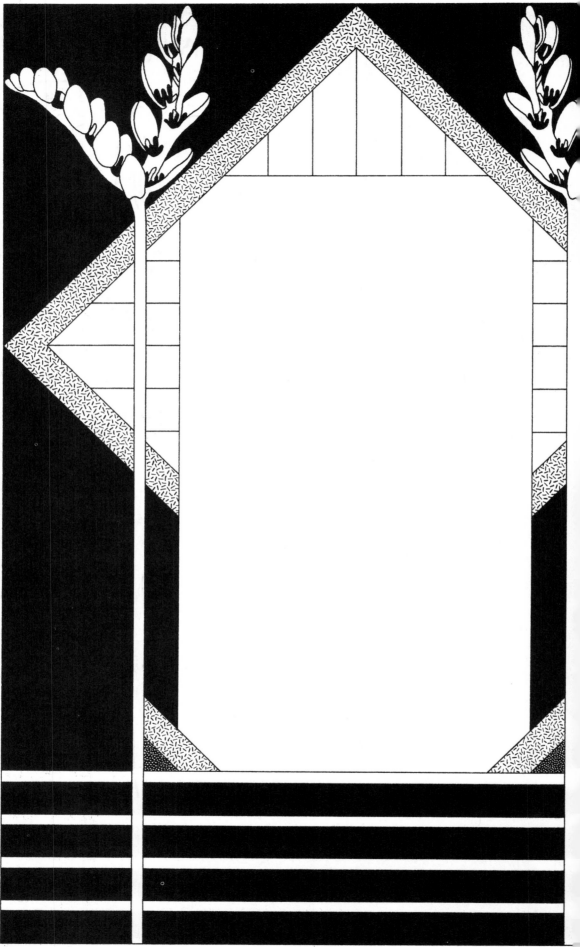

34

42

43

49

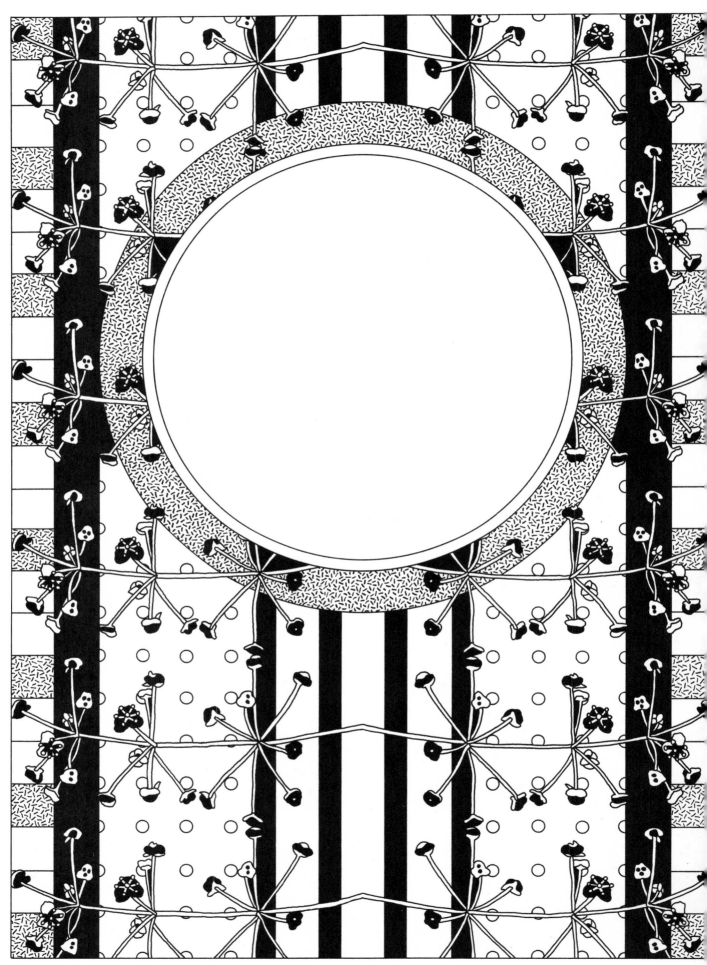

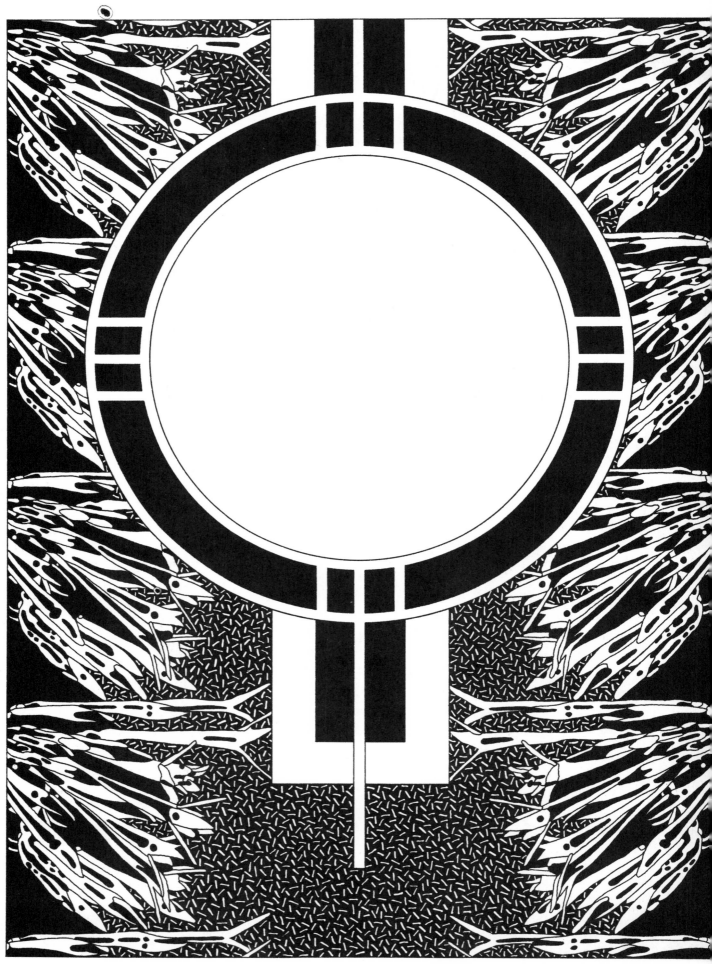